MW01590924

TOP COUNTRY HITS

QUEENSWAY
MUSIC CENTRE LIMITED
701 The Queensway, Toronto, Ont. M8Y 1L2
Phone 259-9723

C O N T E N T S

ALWAYS ON MY MIND . . . . Willie Nelson 35
BEHIND CLOSED DOORS . . . . Charlie Rich 11
BOOT SCOOTIN' BOOGIE . . . . . . Brooks & Dunn 3
BYE BYE, LOVE . . . . The Everly Brothers 26
COULD'VE BEEN ME . . . . Billy Ray Cyrus 40
CRYING . . . . Roy Orbison 14
DON'T UNDERESTIMATE
  MY LOVE FOR YOU . . . . Lee Greenwood 30
FRIENDS & LOVERS (Both To Each Other) . Juice Newton & Eddie Rabbitt . . . 4
I BELIEVE IN MUSIC . . . . Mac Davis 10
I SANG DIXIE . . . . Dwight Yoakam 21
I'LL STILL BE LOVING YOU . . . . . . Restless Heart 36
A LONG AND LASTING LOVE . . . . . Crystal Gayle 15
LOST IN THE FIFTIES TONIGHT
  (In The Still Of The Night) . . . . . Ronnie Milsap 25
LOVE, ME . . . . Collin Raye 22
MOUNTAIN MUSIC . . . . Alabama 6
MR. BOJANGLES . . . . Jerry Jeff Walker 13
OH, PRETTY WOMAN . . . . Roy Orbison 32
PUT YOUR HAND IN THE HAND . . . . Anne Murray 16
RHINESTONE COWBOY . . . . . . Glen Campbell 20
RICOCHET ROMANCE . . . . Teresa Brewer 12
SINCE I FELL FOR YOU . . . . Charlie Rich 38
(YOU'RE MY) SOUL AND INSPIRATION . The Oak Ridge Boys 24
THE SWEETEST THING (I've Ever Known) . Juice Newton 27
TAKE THIS JOB AND SHOVE IT . . . . Johnny Paycheck 19
TIME IN A BOTTLE . . . . Jim Croce 18
WAKE UP, LITTLE SUSIE . . . . The Everly Brothers 28
WHERE'VE YOU BEEN . . . . Kathy Mattea 34
WILDFIRE . . . . Michael Martin Murphey 43
THE WIND BENEATH MY WINGS . . . Gary Morris 8
THE YELLOW ROSE OF TEXAS . . . . Mitch Miller 42

BOOT SCOOTIN' BOOGIE

Words and Music by
RONNIE DUNN

FRIENDS & LOVERS
(Both To Each Other)

Words and Music by
PAUL GORDON and JAY GRUSKA

5

MOUNTAIN MUSIC

Words and Music by
RANDY OWEN

THE WIND BENEATH MY WINGS
FROM THE ORIGINAL MOTION PICTURE SOUNDTRACK "BEACHES"

Words and Music by
LARRY HENLEY and JEFF SILBAR

I BELIEVE IN MUSIC

Words and Music by
MAC DAVIS

BEHIND CLOSED DOORS

Words & Music by
KENNY O'DELL

RICOCHET ROMANCE

Words and Music by
LARRY COLEMAN, JOE DARION
and NORMAN GIMBEL

MR. BOJANGLES

Words and Music by
JERRY JEFF WALKER

CRYING

Words and Music by
ROY ORBISON and JOE MELSON

Moderately slow, with feeling

A LONG AND LASTING LOVE

Words by GERRY GOFFIN
and MICHAEL MASSER

Music by MICHAEL MASSER

PUT YOUR HAND IN THE HAND

Words and Music by
GENE MacLELLAN

TIME IN A BOTTLE

Words and Music by
JIM CROCE

TAKE THIS JOB AND SHOVE IT

Words and Music by
DAVID ALLEN COE

RHINESTONE COWBOY

Words and Music by
LARRY WEISS

I SANG DIXIE

Words and Music by
DWIGHT YOAKAM

LOVE, ME

Words and Music by
MAX T. BARNES and SKIP EWING

(YOU'RE MY) SOUL AND INSPIRATION

Words and Music by
BARRY MANN and CYNTHIA WEIL

LOST IN THE FIFTIES TONIGHT
(In The Still Of The Night)

Words and Music by
TROY SEALS, FRED PARRIS
and MIKE REID

50's Rock feel

BYE, BYE LOVE

Words and Music by
BOUDLEAUX BRYANT
and FELICE BRYANT

THE SWEETEST THING
(I've Ever Known)

Words and Music by
OTHA YOUNG

WAKE UP LITTLE SUSIE

Words and Music by
BOUDELEAUX BRYANT and FELICE BRYANT

DON'T UNDERESTIMATE MY LOVE FOR YOU

Words and Music by
STEVE DIAMOND, STEVE DORFF
and DAVE LOGGINS

Slowly, in 2

OH, PRETTY WOMAN

Words and Music by
ROY ORBISON and BILL DEES

WHERE'VE YOU BEEN

Words and Music by
JON VEZNER and DON HENRY

ALWAYS ON MY MIND

Words and Music by
WAYNE THOMPSON, MARK JAMES
and JOHNNY CHRISTOPHER

I'LL STILL BE LOVING YOU

Words and Music by
PAT BUNCH, PAM ROSE,
MARY ANN KENNEDY & TODD CERNEY

Moderately

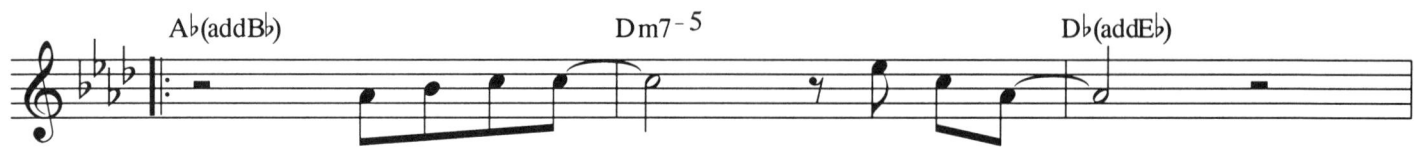

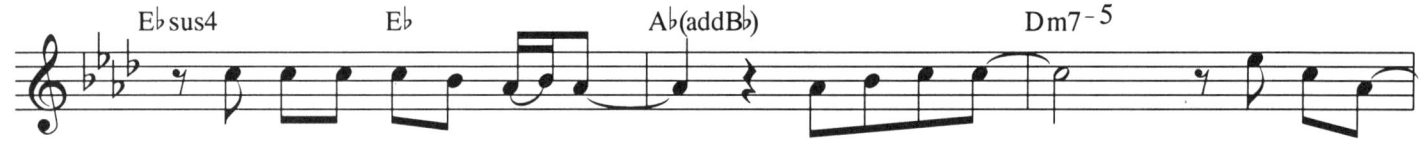

SINCE I FELL FOR YOU

Words and Music by
BUDDY JOHNSON

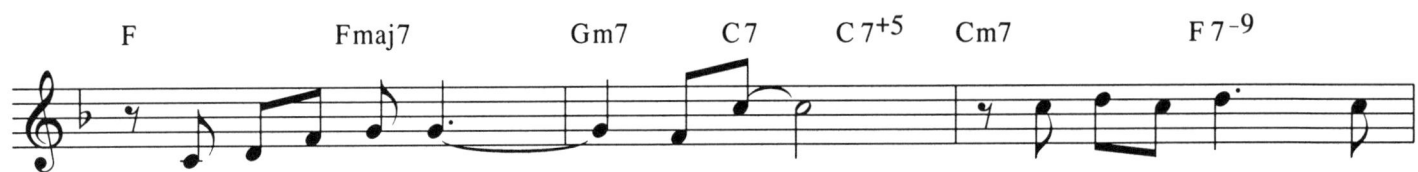

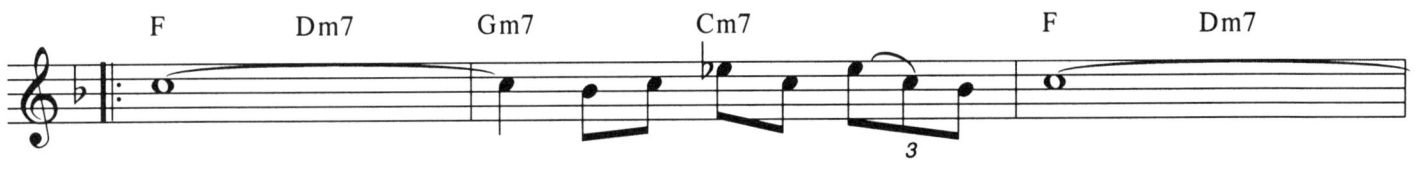

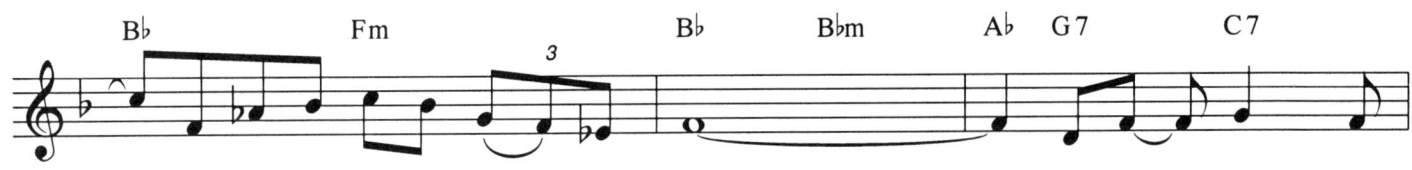

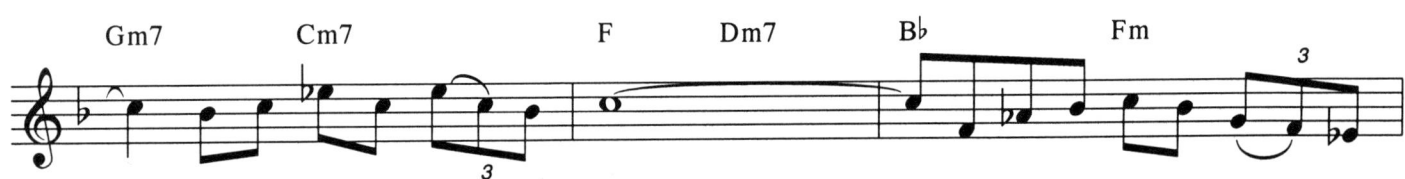

COULD'VE BEEN ME

Words and Music by
MONTY POWELL and REED NIELSEN

THE YELLOW ROSE OF TEXAS

Words and Music by
DON GEORGE

WILDFIRE

Words by MICHAEL MARTIN MURPHEY

Music by LARRY CANSLER